WHY DO VOLCANOES BLOW THEIR TOPS?

Questions and Answers About Volcanoes and Earthquakes

BY MELVIN AND GILDA BERGER
ILLUSTRATED BY HIGGINS BOND

SCHOLASTIC
REFERENCE

CONTENTS

KEY TO ABBREVIATIONS

cm = centimeter / centimetre
kg = kilogram
km = kilometer / kilometre
km^2 = square kilometer / kilometre
m = meter / metre
°C = degrees Centigrade

Text copyright © 1999 by Melvin Berger and Gilda Berger
Illustrations copyright © 1999 by Barbara Higgins Bond
All rights reserved. Published by Scholastic Inc.
SCHOLASTIC and associated logos are trademarks and/or registered trademarks of
Scholastic Inc.

No part of this publication may be reproduced, or stored in a retrieval system, or
transmitted in any form or by any means, electronic, mechanical, photocopying,
recording, or otherwise, without written permission of the publisher. For information
regarding permission, write to Scholastic Inc., Attention: Permissions Department, 555
Broadway, New York, NY 10012.

ISBN 0-439-09581-6

Book design by David Saylor and Nancy Sabato

10 9 8 7 6 5 4 3 2 1   9/9 0/0 01 02 03

Printed in the U.S.A.   08
First printing, October 1999

Expert reader: Paul Vetter, Ph.D.
Staff Scientist
E.O. Lawrence Berkeley National Laboratory
Berkeley, CA

For Jacki Itchkow and the boys and girls in her class
— M. AND G. BERGER

To another great and powerful force of nature,
my mother, Mrs. Edna Higgins North
— HIGGINS BOND

INTRODUCTION

Volcanoes and earthquakes always seem to go together. For many years, scientists wondered why volcanoes and earthquakes are neighbors. Then, around 1970, they began to solve the mystery.

The entire surface of the earth is made up of about 12 major plates, or pieces, and several smaller plates. These plates form Earth's crust. In some places the rocky plates reach up very high. These are the continents. In other places, the rock is low, forming basins that are filled with water. These are the oceans.

The plates are like huge rafts of rock. Some plates are pushing against each other. Others are rubbing against each other. And still others are pulling away from each other.

As the plates push, slide, or pull apart, amazing things happen. Volcanoes erupt and earthquakes shake the land along the edges!

As you read this book, you'll discover the whys and hows, wheres and whens of volcanoes and earthquakes. The facts are sure to astound you!

Melvin Berger

Gilda Berger

VOLCANOES—WHY AND HOW

Why do volcanoes blow their tops?

Because they erupt with such tremendous force. The force can knock the top off a mountain!

The volcano's force comes from deep within the earth. It is so hot at our planet's core that rock melts. Melted rock becomes thick, mushy magma. The great heat makes the magma expand. It rises and collects in an underground pool.

Solid rock presses hard against the pool of magma. The pressure forces magma into cracks in the rock. Suddenly, the magma finds a way up to the earth's surface. BOOM! The melted rock blasts out of the ground. Another volcano blows its top!

How hot is it inside the earth?

Very hot. And the farther down you go, the hotter it gets. A few miles (kilometers) within the earth, temperatures may reach as high as 1,600 degrees Fahrenheit (870ºC). That's much hotter than your oven at home—and hot enough to melt rock into magma.

Does all rock melt?

No. Only the edges of the plates that make up the earth's crust melt.

When two plates push against each other, one of the plates may be forced under the other. Down, down it slides to where it's hot enough to melt rock. The edge of the plate melts and becomes magma.

Magma pool

Earth's core

What makes a volcano erupt?

Pressure. It pushes on the underground pool of magma. The magma bursts through to the surface. The explosion is like toothpaste shooting out of a tube when you give it a hard squeeze.

Also, the magma is filled with bubbly gases. These gases make a mighty fountain that helps blast out the magma. It is just like liquid squirting out when you pop the cap off a bottle of warm, shaken soda.

When magma reaches the earth's surface, it becomes lava.

What is the difference between lava and magma?

None. Lava is magma after it hits the air. It comes out as a red-hot liquid. Later the lava cools and becomes solid.

What else do volcanoes spit out?

Pieces of rock called tephra (TEHF-ruh). Tephra is magma that hardened under the surface or after being sprayed from the volcano.

Tiny bits of tephra form volcanic dust. Clouds of dust from a big volcano turn the sky black and reduce the amount of sunlight reaching Earth.

Slightly bigger pieces of tephra are called volcanic ash. When the ash mixes with water and spreads across the land you have a mudflow.

Large pieces of tephra are called volcanic bombs. Big bombs can measure more than 4 feet (1.2 m) across and weigh many tons (tonnes). Those who study volcanoes up close wear protective clothing. Good idea!

Why do volcanoes smell bad?

Because they give off gas. Most is steam. But mixed in are other gases. Some are poisonous; some, like hydrogen sulfide, just smell bad.

Are all eruptions violent?

No. It all depends on what comes out of the volcano.

Hawaiian eruptions tend to be quiet and steady. They produce thin, liquid lava that flows out in hot streams called "rivers of fire," which cool slowly. The Hawaiian Islands came from this type of eruption.

Certain eruptions are called Strombolian. They are named after Stromboli, an island volcano off the coast of Italy. Thick lava explodes out in separate bursts that sound like a jet engine at close range. Each explosion shoots blobs of lava into the air.

The Vulcano volcano, near Sicily, gave Vulcanian eruptions their name. Here sticky magma plugs up the volcano's opening. The pressure keeps building until it finally blasts out the plug. The force flings lava, gas, rock, and dust high into the air and over large areas.

Peléean eruptions take their name from Mount Pelée on the island of Martinique. They are the wildest of all. Huge amounts of lava, hot gas, and ash shoot out of the top and sides of the volcano. A killer cloud of hot gas, ash, and rocks races down the mountain and across the land at speeds up to 150 miles (240 km) an hour.

Strombolian eruption

Vulcanian eruption

Peléean eruption

Do all volcanoes look alike?

No. Some volcanoes build up from many slow, steady, separate flows of near-liquid lava. The flows form giant volcanoes, low and broad in shape, with very gentle slopes. Since they look like ancient shields, they are called shield volcanoes. The largest volcano on Earth is Mauna Loa, a shield volcano in Hawaii.

Cinder cone volcanoes form when solid rock and ash shoot up into the air and fall back around the volcano opening. Many layers of rock and ash pile up to form a mountain with steeply sloped sides that looks like an upside-down ice-cream cone. Sunset Crater in Arizona is a cinder cone volcano.

Composite volcanoes are also called strato volcanoes. Sometimes these volcanoes erupt with molten lava, sometimes with solid rocks and ash. The material forms alternating layers that create towering volcanoes. The shape is probably most like the one that comes to mind when you think of a volcano. The very beautiful Mount Fuji in Japan, with its snow-covered top, is a perfect example of a composite volcano.

Shield volcano

Cinder cone volcano

Composite volcano

How often do volcanoes erupt?

Always, sometimes, or never. Volcanoes that keep erupting are called active. Stromboli is an active volcano. The constant glow of its lava gives Stromboli the nickname "Lighthouse of the Mediterranean."

Volcanoes that have not erupted for a while, but which may erupt again, are said to be dormant. Paricutín in Mexico is a dormant volcano. It has not erupted since 1952.

Volcanoes that have not erupted for thousands of years are called extinct. They will probably never erupt again. The city of Edinburgh, Scotland, is built around an extinct volcano. At least, we hope it's extinct!

What do you find at the top of volcanoes?

Openings called craters. Most craters measure a few feet (meters) to 1 mile (1.6 km) across and as much as 2,000 feet (600 m) deep.

When part of the volcano top collapses, it forms a caldera. *Caldera* is Spanish for "kettle." A caldera is usually more than 1 mile (1.6 km) wide. Craters and calderas often fill with water and become lakes. In spite of its name, Crater Lake in Oregon is really a caldera. It is about 6 miles (10 km) across and 1,932 feet (589 m) deep. Quite a kettle!

Where are volcanoes found?

On every continent—except Australia. But more than half of the world's volcanoes are in the "Ring of Fire," a broad zone all around the Pacific Ocean.

The Ring of Fire marks where the Pacific plate meets the Eurasian and Indian-Australian plates in the west and the North American and South American plates in the east. The map on page 37 shows the Ring of Fire.

You can also find many volcanoes near the Mediterranean Sea. Here the Eurasian plate meets the African and Arabian plates. Another site is around the Caribbean Sea. The North American plate and the Caribbean plate come together here.

▲ Crater

▼ Caldera

Do volcanoes erupt under the sea?

Yes indeed. In fact, many more volcanoes may erupt underwater than erupt on land. They are called rift volcanoes.

Rift volcanoes occur where two plates are pulling apart, usually between 1 and 2 miles (1.6 and 3.2 km) below sea level. These volcanoes form as magma oozes up between the two plates. The magma fills in the gap, pushing the plates farther apart.

Rift volcanoes pop up under the Atlantic Ocean. The North American plate and the Eurasian plate are slowly separating. This means the Atlantic Ocean is growing wider! Friends on opposite sides of the Atlantic will be 1 inch (2.5 cm) farther apart next year.

Where else do volcanoes erupt?

Over "hot spots," which are rising columns of magma far from plate edges. Hot spots "burn" their way up through the plate. Volcanoes above hot spots may grow high enough to form islands.

The Hawaiian Islands formed over a hot spot in the middle of the Pacific plate. Orginally there was only one Hawaiian Island at this hot spot. Today there are five main volcanic islands. The plate on which the islands rest moves very slowly. It took about one million years for each island to travel over the hot spot.

Is Earth the only planet with volcanoes?

No. Venus and Mars have volcanoes. So do Earth's moon and Jupiter's moon, Io.

The extinct Olympus Mons on Mars is the biggest known volcano in the solar system. It is about 16 miles (26 km) high and 370 miles (600 km) wide.

Venus and Io both seem to have active volcanoes. Io has at least 8 volcanoes and about 200 calderas, evidence of past volcanoes. Some think that dust from Io's volcanoes makes up part of Jupiter's rings.

Do airplanes fly over volcanoes?

No longer. Pilots learned their lesson back in 1982. That year, a jetliner flew over an erupting volcano in Galunggung, West Java. The volcano threw ash more than 25,000 feet (7,600 m) into the air. The ash reached high enough to clog the plane's engines.

The plane fell straight down for thousands of feet (meters). Finally, the pilot was able to restart the jet engines. Since then planes aren't allowed to fly over active volcanoes!

Does anyone live inside a volcano?

Yes. For generations, some people in Turkey have lived in rock formed by ancient volcanic eruptions. The rooms are so cool, there's no need for air-conditioning.

Where do people use volcanoes to keep warm?

In Iceland, Italy, and Japan. Rainwater seeps down into the earth. Magma under the ground around volcanoes heats the water. Pipes then send the heated water or steam into people's homes to keep them warm during cold winter months.

What else is good about a volcano?

The ash that falls to the ground after an eruption contains many valuable minerals. They help to make the soil very fertile. Because of rich soil on the slopes of the Gunung Agung volcano in Bali, farmers there can grow three crops of rice a year.

Volcanoes also bring precious metals, such as gold and silver, to the surface of the earth. Diamonds may also form as the volcano's magma cools over time.

How many people live near volcanoes?

About one-half billion! Still, the benefits are often not worth the risks. An eruption of Gunung Agung in 1963 killed 1,200 people who lived on its slopes.

VOLCANOES—WHERE AND WHEN

Where and when did a volcano bury two cities?

Italy, in the year A.D. 79. Mount Vesuvius erupted violently, burying the cities of Pompeii and Herculaneum under torrents of gases, lava, and ash.

In Pompeii, heavy rains hardened the ash into solid concrete. The concrete buried the city in a layer up to 23 feet (7 m) thick. Herculaneum disappeared under an even deeper cover of ash—as high as 60 feet (18 m) in some places.

Hundreds of years passed. People forgot about the lost cities of Pompeii and Herculaneum.

When did people find the lost cities?

In the 1700s. A farmer digging in his field struck the top of a wall from ancient Pompeii. During the following years, people unearthed much of the buried city.

A peasant found Herculaneum while digging a well. Here, too, experts dug down and uncovered many treasures. Body-shaped holes showed where people were struck down by Vesuvius. Near them were loaves of bread, bowls of fruit, tables, vases, jewelry, paintings, and everyday tools. The findings provided a precious glimpse of life in ancient times.

Did a volcano ever destroy a continent?

Probably not. Ancient legends tell that the continent Atlantis, home to a great civilization, sank into the sea after a powerful volcano erupted.

Today, experts think Atlantis was not a continent, but an island off the coast of Greece called Thira. About 1470 B.C., a major earthquake ripped the island apart. And it was the tales about Thira and its volcano that led to the Atlantis legend.

The excavation of Pompeii

Which volcano was heard halfway around the world?

Krakatau, a tiny uninhabited volcanic island in the South Pacific. The island erupted in 1883. The eruption was so loud that people on islands in the Indian Ocean, 3,000 miles (4,800 km) away, heard the roar!

Krakatau was a deadly volcano that killed 36,000 people. Also, the wind spread volcanic ash all over the world. Hundreds of miles (kilometers) away, the sky was so dark that people had to light lamps during the day. For the next two years, volcanic dust hung in the air as far away as London.

How could Krakatau kill thousands if no one lived there?

The force of the volcano formed tsunamis (tsoo-NAH-meez), or massive waves, that went out in all directions. It was tsunamis, not the volcano, that killed all the people. Tsunamis slammed into the islands of Java and Sumatra near Krakatau. They washed away nearly 300 coastal villages, people and all.

About 12 hours after the eruption, another tsunami crashed down in South Africa—5,500 miles (8,800 km) away. Others set record high-water marks as far away as San Francisco, the English Channel, and the coast of Panama.

Mount Pelée on the island of Martinique in the Caribbean. In May 1902, the volcano erupted, sending a superhot cloud of ash, rock, and gas directly at the city of St. Pierre.

   Within three minutes, the poisonous cloud killed 34,000 inhabitants. Only two survived: a shoemaker who miraculously escaped with only bad burns, and a prisoner who had been locked in a dungeon cell with thick stone walls.

This was one time when crime did pay!

Where did someone see the birth of a volcano?

In Paricutín, Mexico. On February 20, 1943, Dionisio Pulido, a Mexican farmer, noticed that the ground felt warm to his bare feet. At the same time, he heard strange rumbling noises and saw smoke coming out of the soil. By the next morning, there was a smoking heap of ash in the field. It was the birth of a volcano!

Did anyone watch Paricutín grow?

No—Dionisio and the other villagers got out of there as fast as they could.

In a week, the volcano was 450 feet (140 m) high. Soon about 4 million pounds (1.8 million kg) of red-hot lava were pouring out of the volcano every *minute*. It completely swallowed up the village of Paricutín. Within a year, the flow of lava also buried a nearby town. It left only the church tower sticking up above the lava.

When did Paricutín stop erupting?

In 1952. By then it stood 1,345 feet (410 m) tall. Its lava covered 9 square miles (24 km²). Ash from the volcano covered more than 19 square miles (49 km²).

Can you make a volcano model that really erupts?

Yes—and one that's safe, too. All you need is a large plastic soda bottle with a neck, a large pan, baking soda, dishwashing liquid, food coloring, and vinegar.

Put about 4 tablespoons of baking soda in the bottle. Add a few squirts of dishwashing liquid and several drops of food coloring. Place the bottle in a pan and pour enough vinegar into the bottle to cover its contents. Then see what happens!

Pressure inside the bottle (magma chamber) builds up as the vinegar and baking soda mix together and produce bubbles of gas. The gas forces the suds (magma) up through the bottle. Suds outside the bottle (lava) flow down the sides. Watch your homemade "volcano" blow its top!

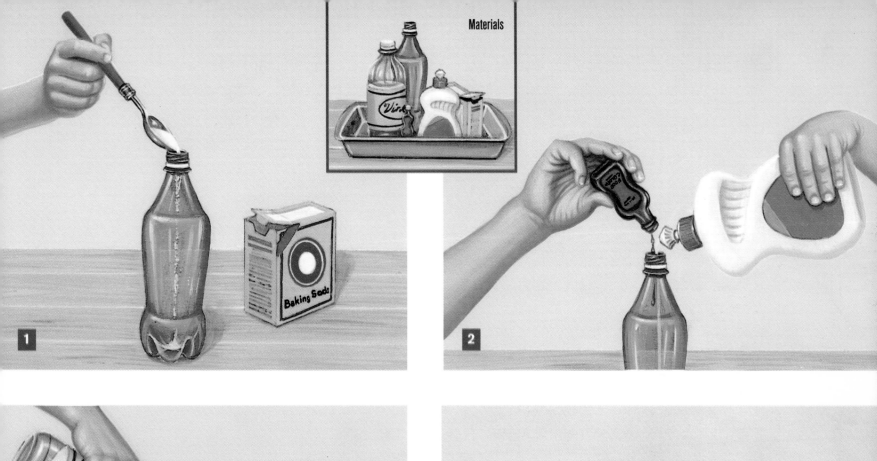

Materials

1

2

3

4

Surtsey

Which is the newest island on Earth?

Surtsey, off the coast of Iceland. On November 14, 1963, fishermen saw a volcano appear above the water with red-hot lava pouring out. It looked as though the ocean was ablaze.

For the next two years, the volcano kept spewing forth lava. It rose about 500 feet (152 m) above sea level. The lava covered an area of about $1^1/_2$ square miles (3.8 km²).

Finally, the eruption stopped. A new island had come into being. People named it Surtsey, for the Icelandic god of fire, Surtur.

What is underneath Surtsey?

The Mid-Atlantic ridge. The North American and Eurasian plates touch here and are very slowly pulling apart. Magma oozing up between two plates creates rift volcanoes along the length of the ridge.

The volcano that made Surtsey probably started erupting thousands of years ago. Gradually the lava built up until sailors could see the island above the surface of the water.

Are other volcanic islands being born?

Yes. Just south of Hawaii is the young volcano, Loihi. At 16,000 feet (4,800 m) it is still completely underwater. But scientists think that it will soon break through to the surface. How soon is soon? In about 10,000 years!

Which island has been putting on a disappearing act?

Falcon Island, 3,000 miles (4,800 km) east of Australia. Of course, Falcon Island is actually the peak of an underwater volcano. In 1913, the volcano blew its top. The entire island disappeared under the sea. Thirteen years later a series of volcanic eruptions built up the peak again, and the island reappeared. It remained a tiny part of the British Empire until 1949. Then there was another eruption, and the island disappeared once more. No one knows when we'll see Falcon Island again!

Popocatépetl

How many active volcanoes are there?

Probably about 1,500, not counting undersea rift volcanoes. Of these, only about 20 to 30 erupt in any one year.

Which is the largest active volcano on Earth?

Mauna Loa, in Hawaii. The peak is more than 5 miles (9 km) above the sea floor and more than 2½ miles (4 km) above sea level. Its base is about 120 miles (192 km) wide at the ocean floor. Mauna Loa is so huge there's room for another major volcano, Kilauea, on its southeastern slope.

Which is the most dangerous volcano today?

Popocatépetl, nicknamed El Popo, which is just 33 miles (55 km) east of big, crowded Mexico City. El Popo has had 17 major eruptions in the past 500 years. The last big series of eruptions, between 1920 and 1922, covered Mexico City with as much as 4 inches (10 cm) of ash.

El Popo is still active. Each day it sends thousands of tons of gas and ash into the air. With millions living nearby, a major eruption would be a major disaster.

What was the most recent eruption in the United States?

Mount Saint Helens in the state of Washington. The blast occurred early on the morning of May 18, 1980. It took only an instant to blow the top off the 9,677-foot (2,900 m) mountain. A pillar of hot ash and glowing gas rose up about 12 miles (19 km) into the air. The roar could be heard for hundreds of miles (kilometers).

What happened before the eruption of Mount Saint Helens?

From August 1979 to April 1980, parts of the mountain tilted up an amazing 320 feet (98 m). This happened because magma was forcing its way up, closer and closer to the surface.

Then, a number of small earthquakes occurred around the mountain. The center of each earthquake was closer to the earth's surface than the one before—another sign that the volcano was about to erupt.

How much damage did Mount Saint Helens do?

Plenty. The eruption devastated land for miles (kilometers) around. It knocked over millions of trees. Volcanic dust choked lakes and rivers. Mud flowed down the sides of the mountain at speeds of about 90 miles (145 km) an hour. Many fish and animals disappeared. And of course, the eruption changed the mountain forever.

The volcano killed about 60 people and forced many hundreds to flee the area. Officials set the total cost at over $2.7 billion.

What happened after the eruption?

Rather quickly, trees and other plants started growing again. Most rooted in the ash that covered the ground. Many animals—from small ones like insects and birds to large ones like deer and bears—came back to live in the area.

EARTHQUAKES—WHY AND HOW

Why do earthquakes happen?

The plates that make up the earth's crust are always moving. They press against one another. Sometimes the plates shift slowly. Other times they shift suddenly. One of the plates jumps forward—or up or down. The whole earth shudders. You've got an earthquake!

How often do earthquakes occur?

About 50,000 times a year—but many more if you count earthquakes so mild that nobody even notices them. They only show up on scientific instruments. About one hundred earthquakes a year cause damage. For most of us, that's more than enough!

What happens in a major earthquake?

Suddenly, the ground begins to tremble and shake. Huge cracks may open in the ground. People scramble to safety as houses and trees fall down. Power lines and gas pipes rip apart, starting fires. Landslides send dirt and rock crashing down over vast areas.

Major earthquakes seldom last more than a few seconds or minutes. But during that short time the trembling earth can knock over mountains, change the course of rivers, or completely wipe out cities.

The largest earthquakes in the continental United States probably occurred in New Madrid, Missouri, in 1811 and 1812. The stronger of them was felt from Canada to the Gulf of Mexico and from the east coast to the Rocky Mountains.

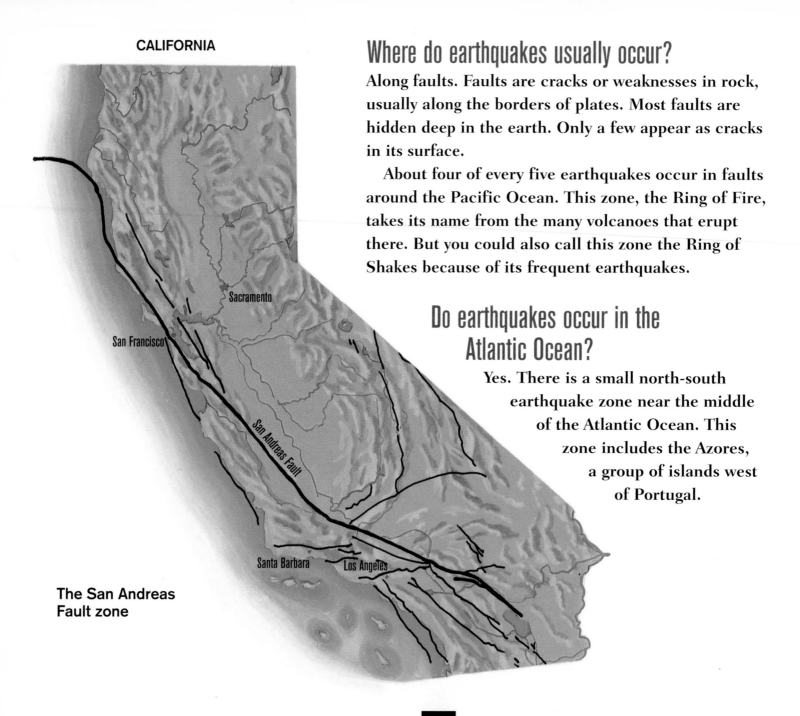

CALIFORNIA

Sacramento

San Francisco

San Andreas Fault

Santa Barbara   Los Angeles

**The San Andreas
Fault zone**

Where do earthquakes usually occur?

Along faults. Faults are cracks or weaknesses in rock, usually along the borders of plates. Most faults are hidden deep in the earth. Only a few appear as cracks in its surface.

About four of every five earthquakes occur in faults around the Pacific Ocean. This zone, the Ring of Fire, takes its name from the many volcanoes that erupt there. But you could also call this zone the Ring of Shakes because of its frequent earthquakes.

Do earthquakes occur in the Atlantic Ocean?

Yes. There is a small north-south earthquake zone near the middle of the Atlantic Ocean. This zone includes the Azores, a group of islands west of Portugal.

What is the world's most famous fault?

The San Andreas (SAN an-DRAY-uhs) Fault. From an airplane it looks like a crack that stretches more than 600 miles (960 km) along the coast of California. The San Andreas Fault marks the line where the Pacific plate meets the North American plate.

The two plates press against each other. Both are also slowly creeping to the northwest. But the Pacific plate is moving slightly faster. It gains about $2/5$ inch (1 cm) a year.

What happens along the San Andreas Fault?

Many earthquakes. In some places, the strain causes small earthquakes that cause little damage. But in other places, the strain keeps building. When the strain becomes too great, the Pacific plate jerks forward and there is a major earthquake.

At least 35 times in the last 150 years, the Pacific plate suddenly slipped. With a giant shudder, it jumped far ahead of the North American plate. Each jump caused a terrific earthquake. The San Francisco earthquake of 1906 was the worst of all. The Pacific plate shot a full 18 feet (5.6 m) forward in less than a minute!

Do earthquakes occur near the San Andreas Fault?

Yes. On February 9, 1971 an earthquake occurred on a side branch of the San Andreas Fault. The quake struck the San Fernando Valley near Los Angeles.

The San Fernando earthquake sent out shocks strong enough to be felt in neighboring states Arizona and Nevada as well as in Yosemite National Park, 250 miles (402 km) away. The earthquake was not very severe. Yet it caused many millions of dollars worth of damage because of the large number of people who live in the valley.

Do all earthquakes occur along faults?

No. Many strike soft or weak sections *within* a plate. These quakes usually cause little damage.

But there are exceptions. Among the worst was the quake in Lisbon, Portugal, on November 1, 1755. It was strong enough to knock over about two of every three buildings. And it killed almost one of every three people in the city.

Do any earthquakes occur under the sea?

Yes. In fact, most earthquakes happen beneath the ocean floor. Called seaquakes, the largest number strike around the Ring of Fire. Other seaquakes occur along midocean ridges. Hot magma rises up between the plates. This makes the plates bigger. As the plates grow and push against each other, they shake the land, and—BANG!—it's an earthquake!

Are seaquakes dangerous?

Most cause little harm. The biggest danger from seaquakes, just as from underwater volcanoes, is the formation of tsunamis. A tsunami from a 1960 seaquake near Chile destroyed whole cities along the coast and left 5,000 people dead. After racing across the Pacific Ocean for 14 hours, the tsunami crashed down on Hawaii, where it killed 61 more and did millions of dollars of damage. Then, it took another 9 hours to cross the rest of the Pacific and swamp the coast of Japan, killing 150 people.

Where does an earthquake do the most damage?

At a point on the earth's surface called the epicenter. This is the place directly above the focus of the earthquake. The focus is where the rock first breaks or slips apart. It is usually between 45 miles (72 km) and 450 miles (700 km) below the surface. Almost all the power and energy of the earthquake comes from the focus.

Horizontal seismograph

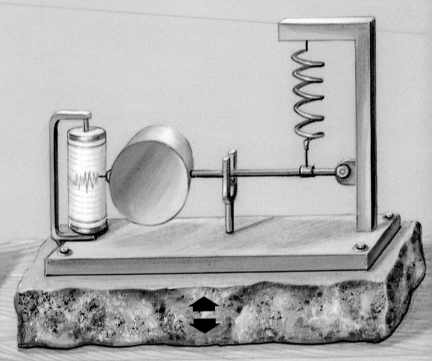

Vertical seismograph

How does an earthquake spread?

Waves of energy, or shock waves, go out from the focus in all directions. They carry the shaking or tremors of the earthquake great distances. A notable example occurred in 1985. Homeowners in Houston, Texas, were astounded to see the water in their swimming pools start to splash. Later, they were even more surprised to learn the cause—an earthquake in Mexico, a full 1,000 miles (1,609 km) away!

How do you detect an earthquake?

With a seismograph. A basic seismograph consists of a weight hanging on a spring from a frame. The frame is anchored in the ground, with a pen attached to the weight. When an earthquake shakes the earth, the frame moves—but the weight does not. This traces a line on a chart showing the amount of movement.

New seismographs are electronic. They can pick up the tiniest earth movements.

Who studies earthquakes?

Scientists called seismologists. They work in more than 4,000 stations around the world. The stations are connected through computer and satellite linkups. Working together, seismologists in several stations use information from seismographs to locate an earthquake's epicenter.

Seismologists use a number of scales to measure the power of an earthquake. Best known is the Richter scale, named after seismologist Charles F. Richter, who invented the scale in 1935. Number 1 on the Richter scale can be seen on a seismograph, but can't be felt. Number 5 on the Richter scale is about as powerful as the explosion of a nuclear bomb. Anything over 8 means total destruction, usually with much loss of life. A reading of 9.5 is the most powerful earthquake ever reported.

How can you measure the damage caused by an earthquake?

With the Mercalli scale. Devised in 1902 by Giuseppe Mercalli, the scale uses Roman numerals to show the effects of earthquakes on people and property.

Number I is too weak to be seen or felt, but shows up on instruments. V is strong enough to splash liquids out of glasses, knock over small objects, and swing doors open. XII, the highest number, destroys buildings, shakes the ground so people can see it, and flings objects into the air.

What happens just before and just after a major earthquake?

Before the main shock there are sometimes several smaller foreshocks. They are small tremors that come before a full-sized earthquake. Foreshocks occur when a plate starts to shift, which shakes the land. Then comes the full-force main shock.

Aftershocks often follow the main shock. They continue until all the stress that caused the quake is released. Also, the main shock may build up new stress in other parts of the plate, leading to more aftershocks. The bigger the earthquake, the greater the number of aftershocks.

Do earthquakes ever occur in bunches?

Yes. They are called earthquake swarms. In each bunch, large numbers of small quakes occur in one area over a period of time, but without a single major quake.

A notable earthquake swarm hit Japan from 1965 to 1967. In those two years, hundreds of thousands of quakes occurred. Most were small, but some reached 5 on the Richter scale. The greatest number on a single day came on April 17, 1966, when an amazing 6,780 quakes struck Japan!

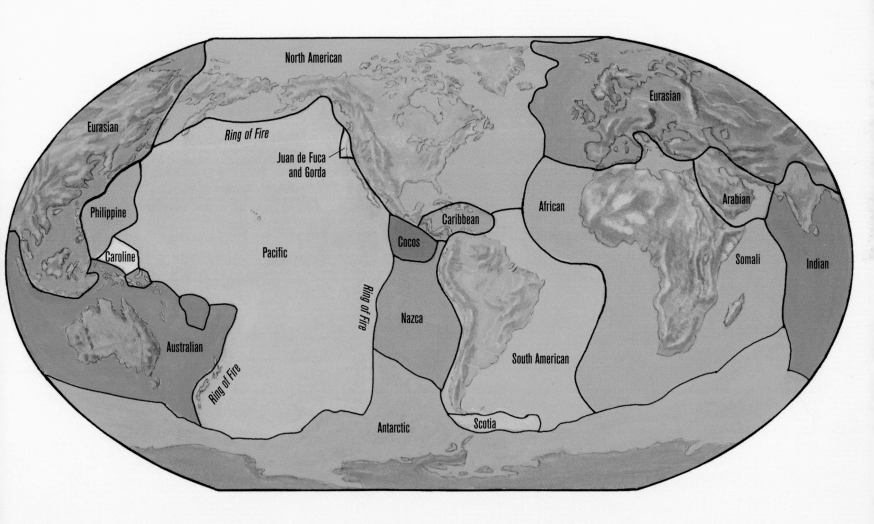

These are the major plates that make up Earth's crust.

EARTHQUAKES—WHERE AND WHEN

Where and when did the strongest earthquake occur?

In Chile, in 1960. The earthquake reached 9.5 on the Richter scale.

The strongest earthquake in American history, however, occurred near Anchorage, Alaska on March 27, 1964. The quake measured 9.2 on the Richter scale. It caused a death toll of 131 and an estimated $750 million in damage. The earthquake destroyed the town of Kodiak. People felt its tremors as far away as California, Hawaii, and Japan.

Which was the worst year on record for earthquakes?

1976. Major tremors in Guatemala, Italy, Russia, Indonesia, China, the Philippines, and Turkey killed about one million people. The earthquakes destroyed the homes of many millions more.

Which country has the most earthquakes?

Tajikistan, a country of tall mountains on the border of Afghanistan. Tajikistan has an average of 2,000 tremors a year. That's nearly six a day!

The city of Tokyo, Japan, is also the site of many earthquakes. Three small plates of the earth's surface meet here. As they bump each other, they shake the ground. This gives Tokyo an average of about three earthquakes a month!

Every September 1, people in Tokyo observe "disaster day." It recalls the 8.2 magnitude earthquake of 1923, one of the deadliest to strike Japan. On disaster day, people practice safety drills to prepare them for the next earthquake.

Earthquake damage in Alaska

Did humans ever cause an earthquake?

Maybe. A major quake struck central Iran in 1978. It killed 25,000 people and destroyed the city of Tabas.

Thirty-six hours before the Iran quake, seismographs picked up a huge underground explosion in Siberia, 1,500 miles (2,500 km) from the epicenter in Iran. Scientists believe that the blast was a secret test of a Russian nuclear bomb. The power of that explosion may have been strong enough to cause Iran's earthquake.

The San Francisco earthquake of 1906

Which country has the deadliest earthquakes?

China. In 1556, an earthquake killed 830,000 people in Shanxi province in less than three hours. It was the most destructive quake in history.

The second most destructive quake also occurred in China. On July 28, 1976, a quake hit 8.2 on the Richter scale. The Chinese government said the disaster killed 240,000 people and injured 500,000, but the figures may be much higher.

Which earthquake in the United States caused the most damage?

The one that destroyed San Francisco on April 18, 1906. The earthquake almost completely wiped out San Francisco. As many as 3,000 people may have lost their lives. Huge fires blazed, destroying about 28,000 of the wooden buildings of the city. The fires burned for three days because the water pipes had burst and there was no water to fight the flames.

During the earthquake, a cow fell headfirst into a crack that opened suddenly in the ground. It closed just as quickly, leaving only the cow's tail sticking out.

How often do major earthquakes strike California?

About once every 18 years. But the rate seems to be picking up. There were major quakes in February 1971, October 1989, June 1992, January 1994, and two in December 1998.

The last earthquake in San Francisco—7.1 on the Richter scale—occurred in October 1989. It killed 67 people, injured 3,000, and damaged or destroyed 100,000 buildings. It also knocked down a 30-foot (9 m) section of the Bay Bridge.

In spite of all these earthquakes, the grinding pressure along the San Andreas Fault is still present. The "biggie" quake may yet be coming.

Can scientists predict an earthquake?

Sometimes. Seismographs can pick up foreshocks. Special measuring systems can also detect any tilting or bulging of the land or the slightest tremor.

Scientists sometimes test well water for traces of radon. Radon is a gas released from rocks under stress. If the radon level is up, an earthquake may be on its way.

As scientists learn more about the structure of the earth, they improve their ability to predict earthquakes.

Where and when did an earthquake prediction save lives?

In Yingkou, Manchuria, February 1975. For about a year, scientists noted many small quakes and some tilting of the land.

The morning of February 4 brought another series of foreshocks. Town officials ordered all three million residents to leave their homes. Sure enough, at 7:36 that evening a severe quake hit. Three hundred people were killed. But tens of thousands were saved.

When did a prediction fail dreadfully?

In early July 1976. Chinese scientists met to discuss signs of a possible earthquake in the city of Tangshan. They decided no earthquake was coming.

Then, on July 28, disaster struck. A massive shock hit the city. It left hundreds of thousands dead. It was one of the highest death tolls in modern times.

Did people ever flee an earthquake that never came?

Yes. A notable example occurred in 1761, when two minor earthquakes 28 days apart, were felt in London. William Bell, a former soldier, predicted that a third earthquake would strike after 28 days. People left London in great numbers. Many fled in boats. But not even the slightest tremor was felt!

Earthquake-proof
building

Can animals forecast earthquakes?

Many people believe that pets and wild animals do strange things before a quake. Prior to the quake at Yingkou, Manchuria, scientists noted chickens roosting in trees, fish leaping in rivers, and snakes rushing out of their burrows. Some say animals pick up smells or sounds that humans cannot. Others claim that these creatures sense more electricity coming from the earth.

Is any animal a known earthquake predictor?

Probably not. Yet some scientists do think catfish may change their swimming behavior when an earthquake is coming. Curiously enough, this ties in with an old Japanese folktale. It tells that earthquakes are caused by movements of a gigantic underground catfish!

Which country has the best earthquake protection?

Japan. Many emergency services swing into action the minute a quake hits. For example, a 1983 earthquake left 844,000 homes without electricity. The Japanese restored service to everyone in just a few hours. Japan has also taken steps to control the damage from tsunamis by building barriers that protect the coasts. And, finally, the Japanese lead the world in making new buildings earthquake-proof.

How do you make buildings earthquake-proof?

Set them into the bedrock of the earth's surface. This lets the building move with the ground during a quake. Also, build skyscapers with especially strong steel frameworks. Place shock absorbers made of layers of steel and rubber on the foundation to help resist the rocking and rolling of an earthquake. Attach small buildings to their foundations with big bolts. For added strength, make some inside walls of concrete with steel bars inside. Finally, connect the walls with steel beams. Better safe than sorry!

How can you be safe during an earthquake?

Follow these rules: Indoors, stay away from windows and take cover under a table or desk or in a doorway. Outdoors, get to an open space, away from buildings, trees, and power lines. Near a large body of water, move to higher ground. In an auto, stop driving, but don't leave the car. Always wait awhile after the quake ends, since aftershocks may be coming.

When did an earthquake move a river?

Just before midnight on August 17, 1959. That's when an earthquake struck in southwest Montana. The tremors knocked off one side of a peak in the Rocky Mountains. Tremendous amounts of rock and soil crashed into the valley of the Madison River. The dirt dammed the river and changed its path. At the same time, it created a brand-new lake. Its name? Earthquake Lake, of course.

When did an earthquake make some islands disappear?

During the winter of 1811–1812. A series of tremors in New Madrid, Missouri, caused several small islands in the Mississippi River to disappear under the water. The shakes were strong enough to rattle windows in Washington, D.C.

Is there anything good about earthquakes?

Yes. Earthquakes help form new mountains and valleys. If not for earthquakes, wind and rain would eventually wear down the crust of the planet to a flat, swampy plain.

Earthquakes also help scientists find out about the inside of planet Earth. Without their discoveries, we might still think that demons under the ground make our Earth shake, rattle, and roll!

INDEX

About the Authors

Volcanoes and earthquakes are two subjects that the Bergers would rather research than experience. Life in New York is exciting, but earthquakes are rare and volcanoes nonexistent. The Bergers would welcome letters from readers who have encountered a volcano or earthquake.

About the Illustrator

Higgins Bond was born and raised in Little Rock, Arkansas, and earned a Bachelor of Fine Arts degree at the Memphis College of Art. She has worked for more than twenty years as a freelance illustrator for major corporations and publishers, and she has illustrated three stamps for the United States Postal Service.